Journey through Salvation

Zenda Galloway

> "Wherefore, my beloved, as ye have always obeyed, not as in my presence only, but now much more in my absence, work out your own salvation with fear and trembling. For it is God which worketh in you both to will and to do of his good pleasure."
>
> Philippians 2:12-13

Journey through Salvation

Published by Kingdom Kaught Publishing LLC

Denton, Maryland U.S.A.

Printed in the U.S.A.

Copyright © 2016 by Zenda Galloway

All rights reserved. No part of this book may be reproduced or transmitted in any form or by any means without prior written permission of the author.

Unless otherwise indicated, all Scripture quotations are taken from the King James Version of the Holy Bible. Scripture quotations noted GW are from GOD'S WORD Translation. GOD'S WORD is a copyrighted work of God's Word to the Nations. Used by permission. Copyright 1995 by God's Word to the Nations. Used by permission of Baker Publishing Group. All rights reserved. http://www.bakerpublishinggroup.com

Library of Congress Control Number: 2016946551

ISBN 9780996404075

Acknowledgments

Wow! First, I would like to say thank you God for every relationship and compromised situation of my past, good and or bad that helped me in recognizing my faith and my call to the ministry of my great Lord and Savior Jesus Christ. Believe me when I say that the Lord will make a way of escape for you.

I want to acknowledge the Reverend Mrs. Herbert who has already gone to be with the Lord. Nevertheless, I find this fitting because she helped me at a young age to realize that I had potential in the things of God. In addition, I would like to thank my Pastor who constantly pushed me to be strong, and to keep fighting and pressing toward the mark: Pastor George Sharps. You were there for my family and me through the tough times, and helped me to look pass the faces of the people when things got rocky in ministry. Thank you, Prophetess Sylvia McMorris, who taught me there is a leader in all of us, and kept me coming back just for her classes. She taught me you do not have to have a title to be a leader and when you are wrong how to eat humble pie. I love you.

Also, I want to thank my present pastors, Bishop, and the First Lady, who are my mentors in Christ. It has been a tough road of adjustment. You have taught me to face the elephant in the room; to have healthy confrontations that I must maintain self-control when facing my past. I knew from the first day we met that you were my spiritual parents, and the First Lady became my mentor. Thank you for not giving up on me. To the Kingdom Celebration Center (KCC) Executive team who is always encouraging and sharing in teachable moments: Thank you!

To my friends, Minister Jamice Holley, Samantha Payne, and Natalie Degraffinreaidt, we have crossed some rugged roads as friends, but God has a way of correcting wrongs and making you stand on your own two feet. We have weathered the storm. I love you ladies. Each of you in your own way has pushed me into seeing who God intended me to be after removing the filth in my life. To the Acklins and my in-laws, Pastor Melvin and Sandra Dickens, who were there for me during my late night any hour panic attacks: Thank you.

I thank the members of my family. Mom, I thank God for the restoration of our relationship. Thank you for being my listening ear. I thank my sister, Keysha, my bestie, who constantly heard all my complaining, yet never got tired of being there. My baby girl, Tyianna Contee, mommy loves you more than you know and I am looking forward to reading your masterpiece.

Lastly, I thank my husband of 15 years. We are overcomers. We faced many things in our marriage and, yet we are still here because of God's grace and mercy. Thank you for sticking with me in my unsaved and now my saved life. I have been through so much, and you have taken most of the blows in the process while I have worked out my salvation. You have always accepted who I am, and in spite of our tough moments, you never left me and for that, I say thank you. You are the love of my life and my best friend.

To God Be the Glory!

Table of Contents

Walls 1
Introduction 3
Understanding the Importance in Receiving Jesus Christ
    Salvation? 9
    Confession 17
    Repentance 25
Faith 31
What's Needed! 41
    Change Starts in the MIND 49
    Forgiveness 55
    Trusting God 61
Ask Yourself? 67
    How to Maintain Self-discipline 71
Tell Yourself!
    Fight for It...Just Get to Him! 79
Citations 83
About the Author 85

Walls

Walls around me
Wall rising up

In my own home
There's walls within walls

But why am I bewildered
Why am I being confined
In these walls

What do I do in
A place of walls?

Do I sit and reminisce
On how I got here?

Or do I continue to fight
Fight like the army in Jericho?

Do I march around within,
These walls?

Praise God!
Or sulk in it all

Walls…
Walls are rising everyday

Where do I run?
No place to hide
Where do I stay?

Bouncing off the walls
In my mind
Falling to the floor

Walls continue to play…
Continuing to play on my mind
The source of this pain
This shame, the feeling
That I am wrapped up in guilt
That was strategically planted
Deep in my mindset
Before the walls began to grow

Wall all around me
Am constantly looking here and there
Searching for a window
A place far off so I can stare

Horizons and blue skies
A face in the clouds to remind me
You're not alone!
Then one day!
My walls begin to crumble
My walls are coming down

Rejoice! Rejoice!
I can hear the trumpet sound
The trumpets that are from heaven
Where I am no longer bound

Journey through Salvation

He heard my cry
I am free
Free from the walls
That once had me captive

He saved me
He paid it all
On the cross
For you and for me

I am free from this world
That's why I rejoice

Trying to find the source
The source of this pain
This shame, the feeling
That I am wrapped up in guilt

That was strategically planted
Deep in my mindset
Before the walls began to grow

Wall all around me

Am constantly looking here and there
Searching for a window
A place far off so I can stare

Horizons and blue skies
A face in the clouds to remind me
You're not alone!

Then one day!
My walls begin to crumble
My walls are coming down

Rejoice! Rejoice!

You can be free from it all
Just accept the Blood of
Christ Jesus the Son

No more Walls…
Satan you lose
With Christ… I Win!

As a way to keep me in bondage
Suffering from the pain
The pain in my mind

Walls all around me

I can hear the trumpet sound

The trumpets that are from heaven
Where I am no longer bound
He heard my cry
I am free
Free from the walls
That once had me captive

He saved me
He paid it all
On the cross
For you and for me

I am free from this world
That's why I rejoice

You can be free from it all
Just accept the Blood of
Christ Jesus the Son

No more Walls…
Satan you lose
With Christ… I Win!

Introduction

Welcome, I am glad you have decided to be a part, or willing to take a deeper observation into being a part of the Kingdom of God. I am excited that you have chosen this material to read and get understanding from God. We all know that walking in the things of God takes patience, knowledge and understanding from the Father, and the foundation that He has laid for us within the many books and chapters of the Bible.

Walking in the things of God will cause you to lose some things and replace your losses with positive ones. It will allow you to examine your heart and get to the root of your thoughts. We should examine our motives and our purpose for everything we do in life. As you go through the different stages of this life-changing process, you may encounter different feelings, emotions, periods of sadness, not wanting to explore some things God has revealed to you about you. Do not be discouraged, His Presence can be with you and help you operate in the things of Christ Jesus the One and only True Living God. I say that because we must have purposed Christ in our lives in order to receive His Presence, His knowledge and His wisdom. We can do nothing of Christ or through Him without first accepting His Presence in our lives.

I just want to give a prominent understanding of the Word of God. There is nothing lewd about the Word of God, meaning there is nothing wrong with having the Word of God in your life. Understanding can be received by fasting, praying and meditating on the Word of God. For a long time, I have often wondered how I can move forward in my life to become the Godly woman, wife, mother, and sister that God has ordained me to be before the foundation of this world. Remember, you will not always receive answers immediately, but know that He is there waiting for those who seek Him (Proverbs 8:17).

I want you to agree to be willing to make the needed sacrifices in your life and be committed to this journey in Christ. Yes, sacrifices! In this book, I want to impart to you the preponderance of becoming a Christian, living a life through Christ. We have a saying that "majority rules," well, Christ is the majority. I want you to be conscious of the fact that Christ should be the majority in our lives. I have had so much bequeathed to me during a short time, and He is still speaking to me. I have not just received understanding from the Word of God, but I know that Christ has spoken directly into my spirit.

Sometimes in gaining understanding and knowledge, we go through so much longsuffering. Do not allow longsuffering to hinder you. It can work out for your good (Galatians 5:22-25). I am just praying that in reading this book God will restore so much positive control and balance in your life. Build on the new things and be empathetic to those who do not know Christ, and share that same understanding, knowledge and grace to every person with whom you come in contact. I would like to see people joined together rather than falling apart. When you

Introduction

realize that we are one Body, yet have our own component to manage, you will focus on growing in your own segment to encourage one another in their parts, as we are all factors in one another's lives. (Matthew 18: 10-14) You must understand that by being connected, what one does affects another, and we have to be sure not to infect each other with the things that are not of Christ our Savior (Galatians 5:19-21).

In the beginning, in disobedience of God's request not to eat from the tree of knowledge in the mist of the garden, Adam and Eve did eat and brought sin into the world (Genesis 3). Now, we are born as sinners into the world. It is in our nature to do things contrary to the Word of God (Ephesians 2:1-6). Thus, there is a need for us to be redeemed and we are redeemed by the "blood of the lamb" Jesus Christ (1 Peter 1:13-25), who died on the cross to save us from all unrighteousness! We must do the work that is necessary to mature in the things of Him.

I believe that there are quintessential things that we need to know in beginning our walk to focus on Christ. I will not say that this journey is easy, as you will see later. However, I will tell you that it takes engagement, responsibility and life's testimonies to move you into your destiny.

As a commitment to Christ, I have been keeping a journal about minor to major things that happen in my life. I am keeping account of how God used specific situations to propel me forward into His plan and will for my life. Everything happens according to God's will when we follow His plan. You will know when you are out of the will of God. Being out of His will is like being lost, stumbling through life, and not having things line up with the Word of God.

One of my favorite scenarios about being lost is the story of the "Prodigal Son" (Luke 15:11-32). The younger of the two sons of a wealthy father decided he wants to receive his inheritance before his father was deceased. He finds himself in a far off country and lives as if there is no tomorrow. He celebrates daily the riches he possesses and lives a rebellious life lacking self-control. After he spends all he has there was a famine in the land where he dwells and the scripture says that he "began to be in want." He became a citizen of that country and shifted into the role of a field laborer to feed pigs. He ate the husks off the animals' food; better known as the covering of an ear of corn. After thinking on his situation, the bible says, "he came to himself." He woke up and reviewed the reality of his faults; knowing that even his father's servants have "bread enough to spare" while he nearly perished with hunger. In returning home, the son thought he was only worthy of being treated as a servant. Scripture says, "The father seeing his son approaching from a distance ran and fell on his neck." When the young son repents and asks for forgiveness, the father's response was to dress him and feed him as his son (royalty) and not as a servant, "for he was dead and now he is alive." The story goes on, but we want to keep our focus on the lost son who returned. The father was able to forgive his son and move on with the gratitude of just having his son back in his life. This is also true with serving God. He is a God of second chances. He forgives us as we go to Him and repent from our wicked ways.

I believe that we act in a similar way at times in the Body of Christ. We sometimes get to a point when we believe that worldly gain and riches are more valuable than that of the things

Introduction

in God's Kingdom. We sometimes feel like we are better off without Christ when we do not see immediate changes in being a Christian. We feel like we were better off living in our sin or that we suffer much more being in Christ. The Word tells us that "to whom much is given, much is required" (Luke 12:48).

Know the words and work of the enemy playing on your mind. We are just like the lost son; we want immediate fame and wealth and do not realize that all we do comes with a price: separation from our Father's love. Like the lost son, who saw what he could get and what he could do with his wealth, he wanted it, immediately, not thinking about what could happen tomorrow.

We serve a right now God. He has given us benefits that if He were to take His Hand off us that we would die, even right now. Years ago, if I did not know about what an amazing God He is, I would have been dead. I thank God for just hearing what I heard about the Word of God that it allowed me to be able to call on the Name of Jesus.

I want you from this point on to understand that this walk with Christ is not about you. Your walk will affect more than just your life. God sometimes allows us to be placed in situations hoping that we will make the right choices, and choose to seek Him and depend on Him to see us through. Let your light shine for someone else to see the glory of God in earthly situations He has allowed you to escape. Even in times when we get ourselves in compromising positions, He will be there to make a way of escape if you would just call upon His Name.

I want you to be excited about what God has for you, how your life will change, and the fulfillment you will have in sharing the Word of God with the people around you. No matter your situation or your circumstances, your highs or your lows, things will get better; things can improve with Christ at the center of your life. See, what you will learn are some of those things that have taken place in your past have happened in God's timing. I am excited to hear about your experiences and life testimonies. Feel free to share them at zg@journeythroughsalvation.com. Reference the book and share God's blessings in your life.

Salvation?

"No one else can save us. Indeed, we can be saved only by power of the one named Jesus and not any other person." Acts 4:12 (GW)

Let us begin with our walk in sin. I believe the best way I can explain this walk is to give you a summary as we go along of my own personal struggles. With my beginning walk with Christ, you see, I had been hearing about church and going to the church for as long as I can remember. For years, I had seen family and friends attend church (the building) and hearing the Word of God, yet no change had come about in their lives. I watched as we would go to church (the building), and come home to be cussed out, wanting to cuss, secretly cussing and watching people drink, and fight and live like degenerates. My life as I knew it was functioning like it should for many years, so I thought! I watched people marry, cheat and act as if it was written in the Word to do these things. You could clearly see in their minds that they thought it was okay. I was a victim to the scheme of the enemy, too. See, cheating is not just physical adultery; you can commit adultery in your mind as well. The mind is where it all begins; for example, that look that you took for 3 or 5 seconds too long. In our minds even when the enemy gives us confusing thoughts, we are more than likely to act on them instead of shaking ourselves loose with the Word or asking God for help. We do not take time to think how this will affect us or even others when we believe what is contrary to the Word of God. We know what is right and wrong in life, but we ignore the warning signs when we are not living as Christ calls us to live and decide to follow the negative people and the negative thoughts. God lets us know that we need to change, but we would rather continue in our sin.

As a child I was a victim of incest for many years, though I did not even see it as such. I cannot remember when it started and that it just stopped. For some families, incest is not viewed as unusual; some members think the victims deserved it. In other families, there are incestuous relationships in which members are dating or raping each other. Whether secretly or out in the open, incest is not right. All I can remember is that I wanted it to stop and that if I told, I would be the one in trouble. Even I had done some things to people in acting out that I am not proud of… even secretly dealing with sexual lust (or so I thought it was a secret). Praise God it did not last long, but I cannot even begin to fathom the effects it had or has on the lives of others. Even as I write this book my family does not even know what has happened, and my offenders do not know how it has affected my life. I could hear people say in my mind; "How could you say this?" or "Why would you speak out on this?" I want to bring awareness and deliverance to all men and women. This is something that has taken root for many generations in our families and continues to repeat the cycle until we put Satan and his pathetic lies to death. I was not even sure that what I had experienced was wrong until recently, after having this happen to a young individual close to me who had endured the same abuse. Nevertheless, God has His timing and it worked out for my good. You see I am not telling you this so that people could be hurt, or I could expose some people. You never know where someone is in their life, so I pray that those involved have or will get right with the Lord.

I want you to be free as this is allowing me to be free. I repeat...I want you to be free! We have to understand that in being free we have to be willing to surrender our lives for the life for which Christ died. That life includes exposing all of our hurts, pains, secrets, and shames. I have suffered greatly because I have held it all in for so long that the anger and bitterness of my hurt was frustrating me. I was taking all that hurt and pain and hiding it so far in me that it took the same tragedy of someone else to uproot my own secret and shame. I had allowed myself to live as a prisoner in a relationship that nearly took my life. A life that is free... frees us from all sin. I had always wondered how what I had been going through made me so bitter and angry. I do not want to jump ahead, but I will say that in our situations we have to know that everything that is taking place (even the circumstances we put ourselves in) work the way Christ intends for them to work out when we realize that He is waiting. The Word says that He makes a way of escape for us. God is Love! He never wants us to be lonely, weak, and fearful. He wants us to live a life of liberation and determination.

(Isaiah 30:1 Romans 5:12-21) When we act in sin, we are like rebellious children, allowing ourselves to be used by the enemy. As children, we sang the song "Sign Me Up," with the song lyrics "Sign me up for the Christian Jubilee." That means as followers of Christ Jesus we are saved people (Christians), who have been chosen as we accept the call to be signed up (used by God) to rejoice during any season or occasion (Jubilee). A Jubilee is a commemoration of an occasion or achievement, so every day is a day of Jubilee (rejoicing) (Psalms 150).

Over the course of this message, please be sure to reflect on your life and how your sin has affected you and others. It is also important to consider how the sins of others have affected you. Why? In order to live a free life, we must forgive those who transgress against us (Matthew 6:9-14). However, that is a chapter of its own. I just want you to understand that in sin we are lost just like "The Prodigal or Lost Son" and that we are made free through the Word of God (John 8:31-42). The bible says, "Faith comes by hearing and hearing through the Word of God" (Romans 10:17). We are to take what we hear and use it to work out our salvation through Christ Jesus (Ephesians 2:10).

When we are in front of God on the Day of Judgment, He is going to ask us to give an account of our life, good and bad, our actions, reactions, and our words along with the many challenges we have faced.

Let us now define the word "Salvation." 1Dictionary.com lists it as "deliverance from the power and penalty of sin; redemption." Easton's Bible dictionary says, "This word is used for the deliverance of the Israelites from the Egyptians" (Exodus 14:13), and of deliverance generally from evil or danger. In the

New Testament it is specially used with reference to the great deliverance wrought out by Jesus Christ from the guilt and the pollution of sin, "the great salvation" (Hebrews. 2:3).

Salvation is the total work of God in affecting a right relationship between mankind and Himself. I believe that sums it up.

However, just because you have said that you accept Christ does not mean He lives within you. You have to purpose it in your heart and begin to walk in it (II Timothy 2:15). The Word gives us specific instructions on how to live a beneficial life in Christ Jesus. John 10:26-29 says if we accept the call and hear the Voice of the Lord, we must understand that we are accepting the commitment to Him that we will change and do what's right according to His Word. We must be active members in participating in the activities of the ministry as God has gifted us to do. We must go to church and join a ministry because we need someone to keep us accountable. Some have gone to church for years and believe that if they are faithful in attending that that is all they need to do. This walk is not easy, and we should not think that we can do it alone. The Son, Jesus Christ has allowed His Spirit to dwell within us in order to give us understanding, and lead us down the path of righteousness. Change! What is your lifestyle saying? What has changed about you that made you so different from the day you thought you committed yourself to Christ? Do not misunderstand; complete change does not happen overnight and not everyone knows how to make the change.

The first thing that should be different is your mindset. People will try to convince you that you are not changing. Your desires may still be the same, but the need for Him in your life will cause you to change.

Romans 8:10 says, "If Christ be in you, the body is dead because of sin; but the Spirit is life because of righteousness." One main important part to understanding Salvation is that when Christ ascended into heaven and when He returned unto the disciples He imparted to them His Holy Spirit that lives on the inside of them (us) to convict us of our unrighteousness (wrong doings). We have been changed because Christ's Spirit should be leading us and our old sinful existence should be done away with.

Jesus did not fall victim to the devil in the wilderness. He stood on every Word of God in order for Him to make it through during those times of temptation. He is our example and we are to do the same.

Scriptures show how God is mindful of us. Exodus 14 refers to the passage of the Red Sea, but what sticks out in my mind is verse 14 "The Lord shall fight for you, and ye shall hold your peace." As you will see the battles we face are not natural wars fought with swords and guns (Ephesians 6:12). Our battles are fought by using what God has given us through His Word and through His Spirit leading us. The fact is that "the hairs on your head are numbered" (Luke 12:7) and that you are more valuable than the sparrows. In Ephesians 1:3-23 Paul speaks about the blessings of being in Christ. This is just one of the many scriptures where God shows His love for His people.

In working out your Salvation, we must remember that it is not about us. I continually say that because your life affects the lives of others and so on and so on. We must understand that we ought to give up our life of sin no matter what it takes to move forward. We must give it up in order to gain the promises of God. In the quest to die daily of our sins, we gain the knowledge of God's Will and Purpose for our lives when we absorb His Word.

Remember, that if what you are doing is not warranting progress in Christ, then maybe you have it all wrong. Working out our Salvation is a constant promotion in the things of Christ, daily, if we are obedient. When you are off-track, you will see that there is no growth. However, when your focus is in the right place, you will see the move of Christ in your life like never before. Your daily mission should be to "Pursue Christ with all your being." The benefits in serving Christ are obtainable on earth. However, our reward in heaven shall be greater than all earth has to offer. We should be excited!!

Requirements of Salvation
There are five requirements of salvation:

- ☐ Confession   Acts 2:21
- ☐ Repentance   Mark 1:15
- ☐ Faith   John 3:14-18
- ☐ Regeneration   John 3:38
- ☐ Holy Scriptures   II Timothy 3:15

You may be thinking to yourself, why the Scriptures? You will need these scriptures to remain in God's Word. These are important scriptures to remind you how God feels about these things. He loves it when we rely and depend on Him in prayer and even in scripture.

Confession

"Confess your faults one to another, and pray one for another, that ye may be healed. The effectual fervent prayer of a righteous man availeth much." James 5:16

First things first! You are about to embark on a lifestyle change. A life that can only be fulfilled by the Spirit of God. I urge you again before going deeper into this book and trying to receive the things that can only be imparted to you by the Holy Spirit; you must have repented from your sins by "Confessing Christ Jesus as your Lord and Savior". No one is exempt from this; the Word of God says in Matthews 10:35 "Whosoever shall confess me before men, him will I confess also before my Father which is in heaven." So, this is major to our walk with the Lord Jesus Christ. We need to understand that this commitment cannot be taken lightly. When we accept Christ in our lives, we must understand that the Spirit is forthcoming. It is up to us to receive all that the Spirit has to say and offer to us from God.

Confession is the acknowledgement and making known of our sin. Moreover, when we confess Christ we are making it known that He is the head over our lives. Romans 10:9-10 *"If you declare with your mouth, "Jesus is Lord," and believe in your heart that God raised him from the dead, you will be saved. For it is with your heart that you believe and are justified, and it is with your mouth that you profess your faith and are saved."*

I initially wanted to put the Confession of our Faith prayer in the introduction, but as this is a message led by the Holy Spirit, God wants you to truly understand what it is and why it is that we are confessing Jesus Christ as our Lord and Savior. Accepting Christ is much more than saying a prayer. Confessing Christ is just the beginning, as you will see reading forward; I am not here to falsely add to the Word of God, nor take away from His Word. However, He is calling me to make it simple for beginners and stagnant Christians. We have not begun to live the life that He calls us to live, until we accept Jesus into our lives and know what it takes to serve Him in spirit and in truth. Paul says that confession is made unto salvation, and we know that Salvation begins with Christ Jesus.

I John 4:15-16 says, *"If anyone acknowledges that Jesus is the Son of God, God lives in them, and they in God. And so we know and rely on the love God has for us. God is love. Whoever lives in love lives in God, and God in them."*

We should be glad that it takes one simple step to be able to live a life filled with love. Maybe you are saying to yourself that there is no love in you or no one can love you. But, here the Word of God clearly states I John 4:19 *"We love because He first loves us."* Let God love you first so that you will know what true love is like and so that you can learn to truly love. When you make this confession, please note that you are not the same. Know that you are in the forefront of your transformation. You are now a work in progress. Please do not begin to use this saying as a cliché. I John 5:12 *"He who has the Son has Life…"* You are in a race for your life. Psalms 118:8 *"It is better to trust in the Lord than to put your confidence in man."* We are no longer living a delusional lifestyle. We are now living a life that if you believe in Christ, He will give you the desires of your heart as they line up with His Will and plans for your life. We have to be able to know more than ever that we have made the choice to follow Christ as the Holy Spirit leads us. By making the confession, we activate our faith and believe that Christ is working on our behalf. He is watching over us and He has placed a hedge of protection around us. God has been keeping many of us long before we even answered His call. In spite of the enemy's plans to destroy your life, God's Hand of protection surrounds you and keeps you for an even bigger expectancy.

I was in a domestic violence relationship and I wanted to get out, but the lust and fear of being alone bound me to the enemy. I had no idea that God was making a way of escape that I so longed for and desired. I had been invited to attend a Christian workshop and for the first time I heard Yolanda Adams sing, "The Battle is Not Yours." I had experienced an overwhelming feeling that something was about to happen, and I sensed that I had to get out of that relationship. Though the situation could have ended my life, God saw fit to save me. I had been plotting and planning, but nothing was working. I did not know how to leave.

Months later (after returning home from work on Christmas Day 1994), I had no choice but to run. Threatened with a gun in my face; beaten and tormented for hours; I knew the first chance I got I had to take it. I had been beaten so badly that I could not walk. But, in the midst of the beating, he decided that he was hungry. He stopped. When he went down stairs, God decided that I had to run because my life depended on it. By His mercy and grace, I got the strength to sneak down the stairs until the stairs made a noise. Then I ran to my neighbors' house where I collapsed. Begging them not to open the doors, I hid in the bathroom and called the police.

I have shared all of this because in the midst of my bad decisions, God was there for me. After ignoring the warning signs and giving my life over to the lust of my flesh, He was waiting for me to call on His name so that He could deliver me from evil. He was my way of escape! I am grateful that though I knew Him, yet backed away from being an obedient servant of Christ, He still heard my heart's cry! Hallelujah to the Name of Jesus!!!

I ask you to begin this walk with the assurance that only comes from Christ, a passion and a zeal for the Word of God and life like never before. He will do it for you! He has been delivering and healing forever and He will continue to do it. Trust Him today and watch how your life will change for the better. Journal your transformation and after some time has gone by re-read what He has done and all that He has promised you. Watch it as it unfolds before your eyes. (Spiritual eyes first (Faith), then with the natural eyes. Amen.

Receive and meditate on this. Take a few moments to examine your life to see where you are and/or where you were

Confession

yesterday. Are you living a life of transformation? Are you in need of this transformation? What is your next step?

Repeat the prayer below aloud with a sincere heart. The Lord wants this here so that you will have Salvation and Repentance, so that you may understand what you are doing before you do it. Again, understand that your life is no longer your own. You are about to take on a life in Christ and retire your will and plans for His Will and Plans. There is no trickery or secret scheme involved except you have to read the Word of God (the Bible), and seek God to understand it.

Heavenly Father, I, Your Name, am coming to You as humbly as I know how; asking You to forgive me of all my sins. Father, I believe that You have sent Your only Son Jesus Christ to die on the cross, I believe He rose from the dead and ascended into heaven and now is seated at the Right Hand of God the Father Almighty. I ask You Lord to come into my life this day and fill me with Your Holy Spirit that I may be born-again. I thank You and I praise You, it is in Your Son Jesus' Name I pray. Amen.

Welcome into the Kingdom of God! Secondly, continue to read... Why? This book is meant to guide you, lead you and to inspire your walk! How do you feel as a new creature in Christ (II Corinthians 5:17)? Are you ready to begin to live as Christ has called you to live? What are your full expectations and desires in wanting to know Christ is for you?

You are receiving a lot of information, so feel free to take your time to meditate on each of your actions to hear clearly how God is speaking directly to you. You should not ponder on any voice or thought that is not in line with the Word of God. The enemy wants to put thoughts in your head that will make you question your walk with the Lord. The Bible says in II Corinthians 10:5-8 "We demolish arguments and every pretension that sets itself up against the knowledge of God, and we take captive every thought to make it obedient to Christ..." Now that Christ lives within you, you will be able to establish which words and thoughts are good through the Holy Spirit.

Father, it is in the Name of Jesus, that we are coming to You, right now Lord, thanking You for all that You will impart into Your people through Your Holy Spirit. This work is for the edification of the Body of Christ Jesus, so that the people of God in faith will be strengthened through Your Word. Having Your Word will allow them to know who You are and all that You have called us to be. We thank You and praise You Lord for this first step and how You will through Your Word propel Your people to a greater cause in You, Christ Jesus. It is in Jesus' Name we pray…Amen.

Choose one thing that you would like to change and work on it starting immediately. No one knows you better than yourself and God. Seek Him in all things first. Then ask Him for guidance in your walk through daily prayers and intimate conversations with Christ. He listens to you; He even hears your thoughts. Seek Him first even if you feel that the Holy Spirit is leading you to another source for understanding. Remember, this lesson could very easily expand to many pages of details. This is not about the length of the reading, but the ability to receive that which God needs you to work on immediately. Enjoy reading and re-reading the Scriptures, take your time and receive the message He is trying to tell you.

Confession

Psalms 119:17-18 *"Deal bountifully with thy servant, that I may live, and keep thy word. Open thou mine eyes, that I may behold wondrous things out of thy law."*

REMEMBER: Read, Journal, Pray, Meditate!

Repentance

"Repent therefore of this thy wickedness, and pray God, if perhaps the thought of thine heart is not right in the sight of God." Acts 8:22

Romans 6 talks about the believers dead to sin. The Word in Romans 6:14 states "For sin shall not have dominion over you: for ye are not under the law, but under grace."

Repentance is to turn away from sin and a change in your behavior. I like to look at repentance as an opportunity to be made new. Repenting or asking God for forgiveness for our sins will cause some things to take place in our lives that we may have never experienced or have been too afraid to receive. This is why when we are led by the Holy Spirit to receive Christ we do so right then.

We must obey the guidance of the Holy Spirit because it will not steer us wrong. Hearing the Voice of Christ is like no other. It is not the voice that tells us to do wrong or anything contrary to the Word of God. We know that we know that it is Christ leading us to His Will for our lives. Does that mean you will not have life pains? No...lining your life up with Christ will cause you to bring up some past issues you may not want to deal with. Nevertheless, it is a part of the process. Going through the process is what keeps you from going back and keeps you focused. I thought about some of the things that I did when I used to drink alcohol. I remember the profanity; that no one wants to be called out of the name that God has provided for us. However, so much happens in your mind as a drinker that only when you are sober you can clearly see the damage and understand why it is important for you to stay sober. I Peter 5:8 says "Be sober and vigilant..."

Maybe alcohol is not or was not the thing you needed to be sober from... you might have an issue with pornography, or stealing... No matter what it is, it's up to you to be free from it. You cannot shake it on your own no matter how hard you try. It is just the reality of it all, some things take fasting and praying in order to be delivered from them. We must understand that it is by the Power of the Holy Spirit, which begins to lead us in all things from the time of acceptance until the coming of Christ. If you would just have patience and stay in His Will, you will receive strength and deliverance. Let us look at the Word of God and see what it says about "long-suffering." I Peter 3:17-18 *"For it is better, if the will of God be so, that ye suffer for well doing, than for evil doing. For Christ also hath once suffered for sins..."* And those sins are yours and mine; He died on the cross to save us from ourselves and the unrighteousness of the enemy who is constantly seeking to destroy us. I know you were not expecting that! Long-suffering...I know you may be thinking, "Haven't I suffered enough without Christ that now He lives within me I can be free from suffering?" Well, do not allow this thought to surprise you, or set you back. God's Word is AWESOME. Paul suffered; his suffering before Christ was because of the sins he committed as a sinner. Paul endured long-suffering in Christ because he believed that Christ had saved him. He was now made a new creature. In his suffering people would be saved because he had HOPE; hope that the people would understand. Our trials allow us to work patience.

We work out our patience by not making hasty decisions and moving at a pace that causes us to think about the cost of what we are waiting for God to do. One thing that we all can regard is NOT being so quick to speak and slow to listen, knowing that through our patience much fruit is produced. Yes, people will try you daily, but we should not give up or in so easily. This is why I ask the Lord to give me peace and a lot of joy. The Scriptures say, "Wait on the Lord and be of good courage..." Psalms 27:14.

Think about it! Scripture says in Romans 10: 11 *"Anyone who trust in Him will never be put to shame."* When we do something that is not of God or in the Will of God, we have feelings of guilt, shame and sometimes we already feel like we have been defeated. This is what the enemy wants you to believe: that you have no HOPE. This is called condemnation. Condemnation according to Dictionary.com is "being unfit for use." We know that with Christ through our faith all things are possible. Why? We should not be looking to see with our physical eyes but with our spiritual eyes. We are to see things as Christ sees them. We are not allowing ourselves to do so if we are looking for things that are manifesting in the spiritual with our natural senses. This is the reason why we confess and ask God to forgive us of our sins. Jesus will not condemn us.

With Christ being in our lives now, we suffer for our lives because Christ first suffered. Listen, you will hear more than ever about the things you did in your past, and people do not believe you will or have changed. There will always be one who will tempt you as Satan tempted God on the mountain (Matthew 4:1-11). They will even mention how your future is dimming because of the wrong you have done in your past. That is when it is important to remember that Christ died for your sins and that you have or will repent for your sins.

However, because we have our naysaying cheerleaders, let their words be a reminder to them and not to you. Christ is leading you into a more prosperous future. When you think about your past, it is more on the lines of being thankful and grateful for where He has brought you from and the places He promised to take you to; you have to make yourself available to Him. There will always be those life-changing moments like at a funeral or experiences during a sudden near-death crisis that you feel you need God and want His presence near. But why wait for that? He is available to you now. I Timothy 2:21 *"If a man therefore purge himself from these, he shall be a vessel unto honor, sanctified, and meet for the master's use, and prepared unto every good work."*

We are now responsible for living our lives in a way that will please God; that will bring honor to His name. Not your own name, allowing yourself to be puffed up with praises, we do not want to further separate ourselves from the Lord our wonderful God. The first thing I experienced immediately after I received Christ was peace and joy. We are able to promptly inherit the joy of the Lord as a resolution to our beginning encounter in receiving Christ in our life. We are responsible for not allowing all that we received to go immediately out the window. Let us not be like the sower whose seeds fell by the way side. (Luke 8:5) But, let us be like the sower whose seeds fell on good ground that sprang up and bore much fruit. (Luke 8:8)

During our Christian journey we no longer are able to "hang" with the same people who hold on to things of the past. It is not about being non-social but, if you have become strong enough in Christ, it is okay to visit and show yourself friendly to those loved ones and friends. You have to allow yourself to get enough Word in you in order to stand the wiles of the enemy (Ephesians 6:11).

Remember, repentance is the opportunity that we are given to ask God to forgive us of all of our wrong doings. We must not use this as we use people thinking if we ask for forgiveness we can get it and do it over and over still. Then this will cause you to question your salvation (acceptance of Christ), but we are accountable to God for all that we do repeatedly. Maybe this thing is hitting a spot in your heart that now things are becoming clearer. If you skipped the prayer the first time, here it is for you again. Do not let this moment pass you.

Quick Prayer

Heavenly Father, I, *Say your Name*, am coming to You as humbly as I can asking You to forgive me of all my sins. Father, I believe that You have sent Your Son Jesus Christ to die on the cross; He rose from the dead and ascended into heaven; and now is seated at the Right Hand of God the Father Almighty. I ask You Lord to come into my life this day and fill me with Your Holy Spirit that I may be born again. I thank You and I praise You; it is in Your Son Jesus' Name I pray. Amen.

Faith

"Jesus answered and said unto them, this is the word of God, that ye believe on Him whom He has sent." John 6:29

Ephesians 6:11 says, *"Put on the whole armor of God, that ye may be able to stand against the wiles of the devil."* In order to do this we must have already confessed Christ and asked for repentance from our sins. This leads us into the next portion in our walk and that is Faith. The Word of God describes FAITH in Hebrews 11:1 (NIV), *"Now, Faith is the confidence in what we hope for and assurance about what we do not see."* Understand that though we do not see Christ we know that He lives within us. Know in your heart that in faith, still Christ is ever present.

Pístis in Greek is faith or faithfulness. We know that when we repent, God is faithful to forgive us. But, are we faithful in our serving Him? I had to sigh right here! This hit me because as I begin to reminisce, I remembered that God was faithful in bringing me out of the hands of the enemy on that cold Christmas night. I can remember that on my journey when I was sleeping in my car, and did not know where I was going to eat or shower; yet He provided for me.

I have not been faithful to Him. I have allowed distractions and my past to keep me in a victim state for way too long. I allowed myself to have a depressed attitude, but I wanted to get right with the Lord. Therefore, I tried to work hard at staying focused on the true path. However, when the naysaying cheerleaders approached me, I began to think about what they were saying instead of thanking God that I am who He says I am.

There will be times when those unwanted thoughts come into our minds, but we must continue in our faith by believing who God says we are. In Psalms 139:14, the psalmist said "I am fearfully and wonderfully made; Marvelous are your works." He is not getting any praise for himself, but giving it all to God. Isaiah 41:10 says, "Fear thou not; for I am with thee…"

In Matthew 17:17-23 (KJV), there is a story about the "demonic boy" that was healed. See how Jesus addresses the disciples in verse 20-21 "And Jesus said to them, Because of your unbelief: for verily I say unto you, If ye have faith as a grain of a mustard seed, ye shall say unto this mountain, Remove hence to yonder place; and it shall remove; and nothing shall be impossible unto you. Howbeit this kind goeth not out but by prayer and fasting."

These are the instructions: that we learn to pray and fast and in doing so, we will have that opportunity to communicate with the Lord and watch our obstacles be moved.

You can seek Him, praying for answers to our life's path and guidance in the midst of making decisions, and get to know Christ on a personal level for yourself. This is just one example of how the Lord inspires using prayer and fasting to gain knowledge, wisdom and get clarity. In a particular situation Jesus showed that because they did not do what was required, they were not able to perform a miracle. I believe that is a great reason why we should seek God in all things first. We need to know how to equip ourselves for what is to come; receiving from the Lord is how we obtain the proper instructions for our already ordained life.

Increasing your faith through prayer and fasting will help you see the power of God unfold in your life. Growing in faith depends upon believing that God will handle every area of your life. Having confidence in what He said He will do. Believing in God, or having the faith for what has not yet manifested in the physical. Trusting God despite what can be seen with the natural eyes. If we continue through life expecting things to happen in our timing and not in the plans and Will of God, then we must ask "Am I truly operating in faith?" For example, if I believe God will deliver my spouse from addiction; should I try to find a treatment center or talk about an upcoming addictions workshop? Not without guidance from the Lord; otherwise you are trying to work it out in your own strength. Even if it was something as simple as bad decisions or negative influences, should I call his friends that I believe have a motive or scheme and tell them to stay away from him? No, this again is not trusting God, or having faith. You may cause too much damage to your relationships.

We can nag a spouse right out of a relationship with God if we are not careful. We need to allow Christ to stand in the gap on our spouse's behalf. You can make your request known by fasting and praying to God about the situation then wait for your answer and watch God work. Besides, this could be God showing your addiction of your spouse to you. Possible! Yes, we could be so focused on wanting someone else to get the assistance that we ourselves begin to fall apart. This is not faith! Who or what am I trusting or believing in, especially if I am trying to do the fixing?

The songwriter says, "Where is your faith in God?" Hebrews 10:38 "But, my righteous one will live by faith." This is my prayer of faith: Faith believes in God; faith knows God; faith is trusting God; and faith gains knowledge. Faith gains understanding; faith is waiting; and faith receives from God. Faith understands that "He kept you while you were yet still dead in your sins and disobedience." And He is still here watching over you, protecting you and your loved ones, today. Faith believes He hears your prayers as you watch them manifest. Faith is knowing He will save your entire household. Start believing that through your faith three out of every five people you witness to in a day will accept Christ and in the other two you have planted or even watered a seed. Exude your faith and believe that God will enhance your spiritual eyes (not your natural eyes) to see what He sees as He sees it. Amen.

Here are a few benefits of operating in faith, but the list does not end here. This is just the beginning of what is to come.

- Salvation - Mark 16:16
- Remission of Sins - Acts 10:3
- Access to God - Ephesians 3:12
- No More Condemnation - John 3:18
- Eternal Life - John 3:15-16

Faith

Allow your faith to be venturing. (Matthew 14:28-29) The excitement of your journey should give you great hope, even in your suffering that it is working out for your good!

Let me share a situation with you concerning where I have been. I believe that God has called me to operate in not just a discipleship, but also a deeper calling. Before I accepted Christ in my life and started to operate in the fullness there of I used to suffer deeply from depression. I was depressed as a kid, and it got worse in my young adult years. Though I always knew the Word of God, I never really seemed to grasp it enough that it took root in the way that I thought it should. In the beginning years, I was in and out of the church, attending here and there.

In the summer of 1994, I went to a ministry conference at a popular midtown Annapolis museum. While there, I believe I received strength, encouragement and by faith that my healing process began through a song by Yolanda Adams, "The Battle is Not Yours." I was immature in the Word, but somehow I believed in my heart that God would deliver me out of the enemy's hands. Praise God! In light of where I was, and what was happening in my natural eyes. I believed that He would do it just for me. That Christmas, He did it for me! After hours of physical abuse; a gun in my face and barely the ability to walk, He made a way of escape. I received strength from nowhere, and ran to a neighbor's house where I called family and the police. Hallelujah!! That would be the last time I suffered abuse at the hand of an individual.

Wow, I have a saying, "Don't allow yourself to sign up and be used for the enemy." Although I did, I can sing, "Sign me up for the Christian Jubilee." God saved me! If it had not been for

His grace and mercy and believing that there was a probability that He would do it for me; I might not have been here, today. God is great! Now, I am signed-up with Christ, and I appreciate being used for His glory. I am now bold and courageous about suffering in my faith for the cross. My faith is taking me to new levels and new heights. We must keep moving forward. We cannot let our trials come between that which God is doing in our lives. I have seen times where I wanted to give up on life, and just not run this race anymore. Nevertheless, God kept me and changed my thoughts and the way I perceived things. This walk for me is too hard alone, but "with Christ I can do all things" (Philippians 4:13). I now know that when the thoughts come about me going home to be with the Lord, that will be in His timing. I know that my faith in Christ outweighs any negative experience, any negative thought, negative people, any negative feelings, and any negative emotions. Though it gets tough at times.

Ephesians 2:10 (NIV) says, "For we are the workmanship, create in Christ Jesus to do good works, which God prepared in advance for us to do." I am not boasting that I did it, no, no! For it was through faith that I had to be delivered, set free and filled with the Holy Spirit. Praise God! Your life in Christ is not taking your life but it is an opportunity to be reborn in a Spirit-filled life. Old things have passed away and now all things are made new.

Around February 2014, I made a decision to follow the unction of the Holy Spirit to come to a new ministry, Kingdom Celebration Center. KCC! I was excited and once I had met with the Bishop and First Lady, I felt the connection immediately. I told them right then that I knew that they were my spiritual parents. It was blissful, I was confident in who I was and why God sent me there. So, I thought! Isn't it funny how every time you think you are on the right path God allows you to flow and then He catches you before the fall?

As I began to do the work of KCC, somehow or another my mind went left. I know you are thinking, "What?!" So, was I! But, I didn't know how damaged I was until I was under such an anointing that I had to examine all that I thought I knew. I was hurt from past churches and ministers who did not know how to counsel, and never followed-up. After all the churches I had been to, I allowed hurt to move me from one place to another. But, you have to leave your emotions to counseling and with the same unction that brought you to Christ, let it lead you through different areas of your life. So, with that anointing I received so much.

After five years of not working, I tried to be content with staying home and receiving what God wanted me to do there. Soon, I was employed by the church's childcare center as the church's administrator. Though my administration for the church was short lived, in everything I learned a lesson. See, when you step out in faith and follow that unction it could take you to places and opportunities that you could not even imagine. But, understand that I had to believe that there was something great awaiting me in this new adventure. I had faith in knowing that God had sent me to this place.

Once I thought I was settling in my position I came to the realization that I was making decisions as though I was working for an old employer. I did not even realize it! However, it was not until I was sent on a small vacation that the Lord spoke to me about myself once again. I had a problem with doing things the way Mrs. Palmer wanted them done. I was putting so much effort into being my best that I was not even following the simple instructions. Before starting to work, I knew that this was more than just your normal worldly employment. I had even said years before that my next job would be with a Christian establishment. But, I wasn't seeing things for what they truly were: God was trying to tell me something. It was during my time off that; He had reminded me of my purpose with this ministry. He was showing me that I still had so much to work on. It was clear the mistakes I made. However, as the enemy was putting thoughts in my mind, I was reminded that this test was much bigger than my pride and was not about me controlling the situation. It would have been easy to give up, but where would that have led me? I heard the Lord say it could cost me everything if I left. So, do you stay mad or do you get it right? I chose to go with the anointing, to shut up and do as instructed. It is not always a bad thing to ask questions or to follow instructions. You might say what does faith have to do this?

Well, faith plays a big part. The bible says, "Now Faith is being sure of what we hope for and certain of what we do not see." Hebrews 11:1 Faith would not have been seen if I left this place to which the Lord had sent me. I would have told God, I do not believe it is going to happen. Lord, how am I going to the next level like this? I had to understand that it was working for my good. If He knows the plans He has for me, I have to have the hope in believing that it will happen. Therefore, I went back on time and with a different attitude. Things are better. I have to admit, though, the test was harder to my pride than anything else was. Sometimes we have to learn just to let go.

I know that you are seeking to obtain something during your walk with the Lord. If you want it, you have to be ready to walk in it. Are you ready to have your faith tested? If you forgot about the emotions and feelings, remember get some counseling for that. Nevertheless, faith is working for your good.

Quick Prayer

Father God, it is in Your Son, Jesus, that I come to say thank You. Thank You God, that You have given me opportunities to journey through faith and have life everlasting. Thank You God through Your grace I have been saved through faith. Help me to live through faith that I may be an example of a fulfilling life in Your perfect Will and plan. In Jesus' Name, Amen!

What's Needed!

Transformation is a change in character or condition; it is spiritual rebirth. Romans 12:1-2 (KJV) says "I beseech you therefore, brethren, by the mercies of God, that ye present your bodies a living sacrifice, holy, acceptable unto God, which is your reasonable service. And be not conformed to this world: but be ye transformed by the renewing of your mind, that ye may prove what is that good, and acceptable, perfect, Will of God." It must be evident that we are giving our all unto God by being obedient servants. Offering all of us: mind, body and spirit is a form of worship unto God. "Be ye transformed," is a continual process not something that happens overnight (though for some it does). This step requires us to be mature in spiritual things. I am excited about the way God is maturing me. In one way, I can see God speaking to me about how to handle myself during professional situations. I can see how God has me react in my marriage, and with my children. Taking once dead situations and reviving or renewing them through Christ. He is allowing me to forget and let go of relationships, places and things that do not give Him Glory. Killing the things that I should not be associated or connected with, and it is all for His Glory!

In transforming, we do not get or should not get gratification in watching someone fall or when we see them deal with their weakness. Think about how you are dealing with some issues in your own home or having to face it when it is closer to you than you would like it to be. The Bible says, "For all have sinned and fallen short of the glory of God!" But, does this mean we can continue to be tempted by the same sin? At times we miss the lesson involved or associated with each sin. When we choose to commit adultery and get caught, is the lesson to change partners and commit adultery again? Or does it mean we work through these tough times? Exactly what have we learned? Are you looking for your mistakes and learning from them, or are we now creating a web of deceit where people are taking their own lives and the lives of others because of one's immature actions?

However, we have allowed ourselves for many generations to be dictated to by the action of others toward us, it is time to let go of the old way of thinking. As we discussed before, find a scripture, positive thought, or images for yourself. We cannot allow the words of others to constantly circle in our heads. We should also spend time in worship in order to get a release from our day-to-day worries. I think Jonas Clark said it best "If you do not think right, you cannot believe right. If we do not believe right, we will never be able to believe right." While I was meditating on this, I heard these words: *Transformation requires us to heal.* Words can play over and over in our head; they have had an impact on how we perceive things in our past, which has caused us to feel down on ourselves like it is normal. How many times a week have you felt like "not today?" Somewhere throughout that day, you heard something spoken or spoken something that was directed to you that did not settle well with you. Transformation will cause you to get that right, to confront it in love. Why? Because if you do not you will have problems later and everyone around you will suffer. Hurt affects not just you, but those who come in contact with you if you have not been able to release that thing.

I believe that many people question or wonder about their salvation because they do not see a change. However, just like losing weight or toning your body, if you do not contribute to the goal by exercising and eating properly, how can you reach your goal? It is the same thing with your transformation if you do not consistently and daily seek the Lord. How do you know how to live Holy and become righteous, walking out your new life? Many unceasingly look at or compare Christianity to Islam (Muslims), but there is no comparison; it is just discipline. Moreover, the same discipline needs to be added to your Christian walk. We serve a risen Savior! It is funny how human minds perceive and operate because we tend to want to see results before we get committed to the cause.

As I was meditating on the words God gave to me; I began to break down and process this message for myself. Just think of the ocean's waves. They are strong and powerful, and some of us sit on the beach to hear the sound of nature. But, if you are not careful, what lurks under the surface can be dangerous and ultimately take your life. Accepting Christ and not following His plan can lead us into dangerous waters. This is why the Word says "many are called but few are chosen" (Matthew 22:14). If we are to be the chosen ones, we must be obedient also, walking in belief that the righteous opportunities that come our way are those of God. I said righteous because to some fast money may seem righteous. Playing the lottery, gambling, dealing drugs and offering it to the community in which you are killing is not righteous.

I can see how many preachers use the word *metamorphosis* and elaborate on the caterpillar and the butterfly. See, from my point of view, I look at the caterpillar like this ugly little creature that gets no respect from those around it. Yet the Lord cares for caterpillars; the Lord hides each one and begins to do a good work within it. "Being confident of this thing, that He which begun a good work in you will perform it until the day of Jesus Christ"(Philippians 1:6). The next time that the world sees the caterpillar, they see a beautiful creation: a vibrant butterfly. It has transformed, matured and grown to be what God has created it to be. Strong, powerful and awed for its beauty, but the beauty is not just on the surface, it is through and through.

Let us take a moment and rediscover the caterpillar and the butterfly. We are used to the process called "metamorphosis." As I began reading the article, the first thing that caught my attention in the very first paragraph was "To become a beautiful butterfly the caterpillar must first digest itself." What!? Just take a moment and meditate on that. Some may already know where this is going, but I want you to understand something. At some point in this transformation, we have to break down who we are to see ourselves through the eyes of God to see who we are to become. Our attitude may be ugly now, but somewhere during this process, we have to receive a Word. Or have a Word on standby like what Paul says in Philippians 4:8-9 "Finally, brothers, whatever is true, whatever is honorable, whatever is just, whatever is pure, whatever is lovely, whatever is commendable, if there is any excellence, if there is anything worthy of praise, think about these things. What you have learned and received and heard and seen in me-- practice these things and the peace of God will be with you." Lord, Your Word says, "Trust in the Lord with all your heart, and do not lean on your own understanding" (Proverbs 3:5). Take the Word for the revelation God gives you and not out of content to soothe you. If that is a Word that God has indeed given to you meditate, and ask Him for understanding and Wisdom.

Scripture says, "Therefore, if anyone is in Christ, he is a new creation; old things have passed away; behold, all things are made new" II Corinthians 5:17.

Another thing we I learned about this transformation is how it changes, "a silky cocoon molts into a shiny chrysalis, its protective covering." Just in case you have not realized it, salvation offers you a protective covering like no other. He is the only God that knows you will receive Him, you will ignore Him, and when you will begin to work through patience to wait on Him. Meanwhile, He keeps you safe. It is not a coincidence that the enemy tempts you to pick up the unregistered gun, dares you to pick it up, but it is by the Hand of God... The wisdom of the Holy Spirit interceding on your behalf that you did not. Coincidentally you did not die that time you hit your head on the wall when he punched you and you fell to the floor. The Protective Hand of God! And just maybe like me you were able to hold on to life another day because God gave you just enough strength to escape your situation. Somebody was praying for me, and I am praying for you.

Lastly, just the beautiful butterfly or moth emerges from its silky cocoon or shiny chrysalis. This reminds me of how God hides us in a place of darkness while He purifies us; then He moves us once we are cleansed and strengthened. He takes us out of the limelight and brings us to a place where we can accept His pruning. Though it hurts, we allow Him to shape us and mold us into something that we could never imagine. He does not force anything on us. He blesses us with achievements we could have never achieved on our own. Again, without Him we are nothing. Simply put, we are not able to do above all that we can think or imagine. (Ephesians 3:20 "Now unto Him that is able to do exceedingly abundantly above all that we ask or think, according to power that worketh in us...") He thinks of us so much that He has provided His light within us that we should shine brightly in darkened places. He is purifying us to be just like Him (Jesus). Though we are not worthy of it, He loves us just that much.

Transformation will cause your patience, your faith, your trust in God to be tested. Why? We have to be like Psalm 27:14 "Wait for the Lord; be strong and take heart and wait for the Lord." This was, and at times still is definitely a challenge for me through most of my life. God is developing your character in waiting. We have been doing things our way for so long, we need to learn to wait for the Lord. If we are challenging ourselves in our walk, God will come if we would just wait. I do not want your life to become a cliché by mouthing you are a Christian. Let your actions and your character speak for you. I do not believe that in this scripture the psalmist said "Wait for the Lord" twice for nothing. But, he is insisting that we be patient. He is trusting through his faith that the Lord will show up. We need to do the same.

Once saved through the Blood of Jesus Christ, we ought to see a change in our lives. Make gradual changes and perfect one or two things at a time. You will be surprised at how one accomplishment can lead you into another. How a change in your patience can lead you into less anger. Especially, as you recognize the issue that led you to your bitterness. We will talk more on that in another chapter.

Transformation is your faith and trusting God; I believe it works hand and hand. You cannot trust God if you do not have hope or faith that He will make His presence known in your life. Throughout scripture, you will read about how through faith God has done some miraculous works. We can have these same results; like the bible story of when King Darius hurried down to the lions' den to find that Daniel was safe. Daniel had made it throughout the night in the lions' den unharmed because of his trust in God. I am sure you have spoken some words of courage and confidence in the Lord that His grace and mercy was more than sufficient. That even during some point in your life you have called on the Name of Jesus and something happened. You thought it was a coincidence. But God!

I just want us to understand that in our weakest moments, the Holy Spirit is going to be there to lead us and guide us in all of our righteousness. It is a process that takes time and we should not try to do it alone. We need to learn to call upon the Lord and wait for His answer.

Christian Salvation…no one else has ever died and been raised from the grave to sit at the Right Hand of our Father. The One and Only, True Living God! Hallelujah to Your Name Jesus!

Now, are you ready to embark on this life-changing journey? Great! You have already begun! You are already developing a desire for something new in Christ. Allow yourself to be free and let the Spirit of God show you His blueprint for your life.

Quick Prayer

Father, it is in Your Son Jesus' Name, we come asking You to show us how to let go and let Your spirit do a work within us. We ask that You remove the blinders and allow us to see You for who You are and show us who You created us to be. Lord, as You show us, we will surrender all to You, not second-guessing or wavering in our decision. Teach us what patience should be like and encourage us in all of our accomplishments in You O God. It is in Jesus' Name we pray, Amen.

"For it is God which worketh in you both to will and to do His good pleasure." Philippians 2:13(KJV)

Change Starts in the MIND

Change begins in the mind. We have to be listening for the Voice and Instructions of God; even when it comes from people you least expect. I thank God that His Word says we are "not the tail but the head" (Deuteronomy 28:13). Therefore, we need to acknowledge the fact that we are not animals but made in the image of God and none can compare.

We must walk around daily with the mindset of remembering we just invoked God's presence in our life. Remember the Prayer of Faith that we prayed! We asked God to come into our lives, and (now that we have signed up) we must walk out the steps as He leads us no matter how much it may hurt. If you would just bear the pain, you will see how He comforts us in our worst times through His Word. I had to lay aside everything that I used to do and begin striving for the plan and Will of the Lord for my life. In fact, I am still laying them aside. You might ask, "How can we do this?"

Changing our mindset… acknowledging that we are nothing and can do nothing without Christ. (Philippians 4:13) No one knows the Will and plan of God unless He shows it to us. God has set people in position to assist us on this journey. He knows it is not going to be easy to do what He has called us to do, or to give up some things. Like those things that we formed as habits in our life. But, what you have to realize about God is that there is only one way: HIS WAY! It is just a matter of how easy you will comply. It is such an honor to be chosen by someone you cannot repay. You are forever at the mercy of Him. It is best to be at the feet of Him; allowing Him to mold us as a representation of Him.

Now, because of our thought process we must be in our scriptures daily in order to do this. Scriptures will help us to know what moves we should and should not take. It gives us strength to press forward in correction and in time of need (effectiveness and stability). It takes courage and understanding through the Wisdom laid before us in the Scriptures.

I can remember when I transitioned from one church to another. In my excitement I knew that I was about to soar. I was going to another level, thank You Lord! Then my world came crashing down, or should I say I was torn down to my very core? I was not as connected as I should have been or excited, as I was when I got to the new ministry. I had to forget everything I ever learned because the hurt was so bad. In order for me to move on, I had to do something I was not prepared to do. Something I thought the Lord was telling me I would not be a part of.

Come to find out... it was me; I could not get right because of rebellion and fear. I was angry... I felt unappreciated. Even after I had apologized to my Pastor for the way I left my previous ministry, I still felt some type of way. I had allowed shame to set in due to not feeling adequate according to man's standards. Actually, I have felt this way in my life for a long time. Maybe you can relate to this.

Maybe you have felt that people applaud you (at one point or another in your life) because they feel you have done something great in their eyes. But, when you are on the path that God is calling you to be on, the same people do not agree or applaud. They make you feel like a failure, or that what you are doing won't work. That it is because of what you are doing: you are following Christ for yourself. Is that wrong? Well, even if you feel like that now, change your mindset by telling yourself that you are who God says you are. No one asked them to put you in the limelight. But, do not let your failures be because of what someone says. What does God say? Stop living in the shadows of human opinions and move into the Word of God. DO NOT BE A PEOPLE PLEASER! Your increase does not come from man, but from God. Some are too afraid to move because of fear that mankind will look at them, differently. There are people out there who will not like you because you get more attention by focusing your life through God's eyes. I am here today to tell you to keep right on focusing on God.

Change your mindset by letting God move you out from under man and get under the umbrella of the Trinity. The Word of God says, "Until He humbles your enemies, He will make your enemies your footstool" (Luke 20:43). We miss the first part of this scripture because we like to believe that just because men do not always agree to see what God sees then they are your enemy. Many people stay at ministries because of the obligation to the man. However, if we structure a Maslow Hierarchy for Spiritual Needs, where would God fit in your life if your trust were in man? Whom are you actually committed to? It is definitely serious when someone takes your good intentions for bad. However, after rereading you will see that, the scripture says "Until." This is an example of when scripture leaders and encouragers tend to leave out what really is the importance of a scripture just to soothe someone. This is why reading the Word for your self brings enlightenment. True revelation comes from God. See, God even has a plan for your enemies. They are used as your footstool "until" they get it right with Him. Sometimes you will never see the change, that is why the Word says to "pray for our enemies" (Matthew 5:44). It is only for a moment that they are your enemies. If we are changing our character to be that of Christ, we should be praying that they too will receive His grace and mercy in their lives, and the favor upon them will be evident.

I love it when people talk about what I used to be; remember "used to" is the past tense. Let us make it simple, which was B.C. (Before Christ). Meaning now that we are one with the Father, we have the right through our faith and commitment to God to move on.

As a maturing individual, it may be hard; it was not easy for me, either. Take a minute and think about all the energy you put in talking about someone (gossip). Or listening to lies about someone that was spread just to make another (or yourself) look good. At what cost are you willing to tear down someone's character and self- esteem if that person is already down on himself or herself? What good are you doing? Better yet, as an individual standing before Christ how would explain your attitude towards this person? How have you responded to them? Is it hurting you to be kind to them? Are you waiting to hear rumors and whispering of their failure in return? Pray people of God. Do not curse your own lives by waiting for someone else's demise!

As I look back, in order to change my mindset, I had to walk away. I had to let family and so-called friends go. I gave it all up for the sake of my commitment to my focus (my Savior). I am learning to *distract* the distractions once again with my focus (My Lord).

You do not have to be involved in what is being said about you. You do not have to disagree about what is being said or how people act or will act towards you. However, God's Word does say that we have to love one another. The Bible says this about 19 times in different Scriptures (KJV):

John 13:34, John 13:35, John 15:1, John 15:17, Romans 13:8, Romans 12:10, Galatians 5:13, Ephesians 4:2 ,
I Thessalonians 3:12, I Thessalonians 4:9, Hebrews 10:24,
I Peter 1:22, I Peter 3:8, I John 3:11, I John 3:23, I John 4:7,
I John 4:11, I John 4:12, II John 1:5

Put your focus on God and His Word and watch how you will begin to see those individuals in a different light. You will even begin to pray for them and their well-being.

"If so be that ye have heard Him, and have been taught by Him, as the truth is in Jesus: That ye put off concerning the former conversation the old man, which is corrupt according to the deceitful lust; And be renewed in the spirit of your mind; And that ye put on the new man which after God is created in righteousness and true holiness" Ephesians 4:21-24.

Quick Prayer

Father, it is in the Name of Jesus that we thank you for even our enemies. We know that without You, we are nothing but without the unbelievers, we cannot perfect the work that You have created for us to do. Let our mindset no longer lay dormant in dry places but in the lives of others who need Your rivers of Living Waters, healthy and springing forth with fruitfulness in any environment. We thank You that our lives will never be the same. Our minds will begin to release all the hurt and pain of our B.C. and now we will be a part of the Vine Who feeds us a life through Christ. In Jesus' Name, we pray, Amen.

Forgiveness

"To give knowledge of salvation unto His people by the remission of their sins." Luke 1:77

Well, in ending the last chapter, we talked about rivers of Living Waters, good health and fruitfulness. Well, we will never experience any of this if we are living with unforgiveness, which can lead to resentment, bitterness, revenge and in some cases death. In this chapter, we are still renewing our minds.

I looked up the word "forgiveness" and here are some synonyms that best give meaning to it, such as: amnesty, charity (love), compassion, grace, and mercy, just to name a few. The Bible states, "It does not dishonor others, it is not self-seeking, it is not easy angered, it keeps no record of wrong." (I Corinthians 13:5) If we are in place still keeping a record, we are in the wrong.

What does the scripture say about some of these words? In one of David's prayers to the Lord, he says "For thou, Lord art good, and ready to forgive; and plenteous in mercy unto all them that call upon thee" (Psalms 86:5). The Lord is ready to forgive. He is great in forgiveness. Who are we that we should not forgive when Jesus paid for all of our sins on the cross? If we say that we are Christians and that we have accepted Christ in our lives why do we hesitate to let it go?

    I thought about my own unforgiveness. I questioned my accusers in my head. Why would someone take advantage of a young girl's body? Why would you not want to help keep me pure as family? Why at some point did I feel as though it was ever okay? Why? Why? Why? One of the things you learn about God is that He can put an end to the 'whys.' I wanted to confront my abusers and accusers for so long and ask them that. Why? What happened to you or what did you see that you would want to take something so precious and so important from me that I could not get back. I did not know how this would affect me down the line. Nevertheless, now that I have seen the damage, I want to put an end to hurt, the pain and the curse. I have mentioned some of the things that I have been through in my life, and I personally have felt all of those feelings mentioned above and much more.

    I just wanted God to remove the feelings of revenge for everyone who has ever harmed me. I am not a spiteful person at heart. However, I see how one hurtful thing can lead to many hurtful moments. Not just to you, but also to the people who have to hear your negativity, see the faces you make, and the body language you use when displaying your anger. I saw how going through the incest made it seemed like on one hand it was okay if that's all the guys wanted from me in my younger days.

    As I grew in Wisdom and understanding and sought help, I

understood that for me it had to be more. I had to learn not to be attracted to what would make me unhappy. I had to find a place in my heart to forgive in order to move on. Forgive them and myself. I wanted to find peace with this situation and happiness in a relationship. I had jumped ship when I thought things were going to be physical, yet stayed in a relationship for years with my abuser. Maybe that is not your issue. Maybe, you are on the other end of the spectrum. Have you hurt someone and now you are on this journey and you need to get it right? Do not hesitate, do not think, but be led by the Spirit of God in how to forgive and how to apologize. Eat a few humble pies.

I say that because not knowing or understanding a person's hurt or pain, you never just want to walk up to someone and just expect that they should or will accept your apology. Sometimes one party does not believe that they have ever done anything wrong, or they are simply not ready to face that truth about their life. Nevertheless, in making peace with the Lord it is not about them, it is about you and about your *lack* of forgiveness.

We need to learn to forgive ourselves first; then we can move on to forgive those who have hurt us; and ask others that we may have harmed to forgive us. I think forgiving myself and working through the shame was the hardest for me. In describing my shame, I felt more confused by unanswered questions. In time you will realize that you cannot make someone answer you or even apologize for what he has done to you. You can only find peace in Christ and pray for your healing. Pray that you will not ignore what has happened but find forgiveness in your pain. Ask God to help you not set up walls about the new people that come in your life. Ask Him to give you peace and then you can give responses like, "I've come through it," and "It's between them and the Lord now."

I never even thought that revisiting some of these hurts in my mind would help. Why would someone want to keep reliving it all? But, one day as I was talking to my pastor, she said, "write it down." What?! Then, she began to explain how once I discussed or expressed myself on paper (my feelings and the details of it all) how it would bring a release. I only wrote one letter. After that, I was feeling annoyed. My emotions and my feeling were all over the place! I remembered things I did not want to remember. As I prayed, I secretly cried, and shared this experience with a few close friends and family. "Love does not delight itself in evil but rejoices with the truth" I Corinthians 13:6.

Yes, the truth hurts like heck. I just know that you have to start somewhere in order to be released from all that is bottled up inside you. The Lord gave me this vision over ten years ago, but I never realized I had so much hurt to face.

I am an introvert. Unfortunately, I am not good at hiding my suffering and the disturbances in my thoughts. We cannot even begin to receive the greatness or recognize blessings if we are still overflowing with so much pain. Just stop, take a deep breath right now and ask God to show your first steps. You should not hesitate as I once did to go to your pastor or mentor and seek Wisdom.

Man or woman, just begin to think… "I want to be free." Then, take the necessary steps in finding your way closer to Christ in your freedom. Okay, maybe you do not feel free. I am paraphrasing here but Scripture says, speak those things that be not as though they were, Romans 4:17. Read it for yourself.

Study it; you will see that the very things that proceeded out of your mouth will take form. That is for another book, but start now to speak the Word of God and all the positive things God says about you. God's Word is the remedy for all who sorrow.

Forgive yourself, encourage yourself, forgive others and find peace and the joy of the Lord, which is your strength. Read these scriptures and get strength: Nehemiah 8:10 and Psalm 28:7.

Quick Prayer

Father we thank You for Your forgiveness of our sins. We thank You that You are teaching us to walk out our forgiveness towards others so that we can be released from the guilt and shame of our own sins. Lord, please let Your Word take hold in my life and renew any wrongs that may need to come to light. Forgive me Lord of all my sins. Teach me to love again, help me to break down the walls that once held me captive to the enemy's schemes. Thank You for coming into my life and showing me new things through Your Word. Help me to work out any anger or malice that lays dormant in my heart. I thank You and I praise You Lord. In Jesus Name' I pray, Amen.

Joy Scriptures

I Thessalonians 5:16-18
Zephaniah 3:17
Philippians 4:4
Romans 12:12
Habakkuk 3:17-18
Isaiah 61:10

II Corinthians 9:7
I Peter 1:8-9
Psalm 94:19
Psalm 118:24
John 16:24

Trusting God

"And such trust have we through Christ to Godward: not that we are sufficient of ourselves to think anything as of ourselves; but our sufficiency is of God." II Corinthians 3:4-5

When I am studying something in particular, I like to break down every little aspect to the story as I am studying. As I was reading about Moses, I began to take note about his situation, and there were parts of it that I thought was imperative to share. I wanted to know the story as it relates to me to jump out and catch the eye of everyone who takes the time to read it. I really did not catch some things until I had completed this portion of my study.

The number one thing was Moses' name. Moses' name means, "to pull/draw from." I thought that was funny considering that this story had sat on my desk for years, and all I wanted to know was how it related to me. We know the basic story is found in Exodus 2, that when Moses was 3 months old, Pharaoh (Exodus1:10-22) charged his people saying that they are to cast all the male children of Israel into the river. Moses' mother heard this and she then made an ark and strategically placed him in the river near the banks so that he could be found. Moses was found just as his mother knew he would be. Ironically, Pharaoh's daughter saves him from death, and his mother and sister who were the maidservants of Pharaoh's daughter continues to raise him.

At some point, Moses discovered who he really was, began to change, and ran from his history. In doing so, he kills an Egyptian. Pharaoh and Aaron finds out Moses' secret of murder and that he is really a child of Israel and now they want to kill Moses. Moses runs from Egypt, and establishes himself in a strange land called Midian. He encounters a group of sheepherders and they treat him well. One of the daughters of a man ask him to stay and have dinner with them. He is given the man's (who we find out later is named Jethro) daughter, Zipporah. Moses has two sons, one named Gershom and the other Eliezer. Here is where my story begins to unfold.

I was reading a devotional one day in 2004. It captivated me so much that I had a strange feeling as if I was connected to the story. Therefore, I made a copy of it and hung it in my office above my computer. I glanced at it and read over it from time to time and still I was puzzled by the connection. It seemed like over years when I started to read and research Moses' history I would always get distracted and I never was able to get into it. Several years later, I was laid off my job. It was bittersweet but I knew it was going to happen. It was shortly around that time that I went on a weekend women's conference. At the end of the conference, I heard the Lord say that I would be writing a book. I literally laughed like "how am I going to write a book?" I am not nearly smart enough and knowledgeable enough to do that (Like Moses lacking faith and trust in the promise). Years went by as I was going through my own wilderness experience. Trusting God is not seeing yourself in your current condition without Him, but allowing Him to show you who you are in Him.

I was in denial about the reasons I was changing. I was depressed and my heart was hardening. How could I get through this turmoil in life through the stares and backlash after I complete this book? But, it was all me working out my salvation through Christ.

God has allowed certain people to enter into our lives whether it is for a lifetime or a short period of time. I have had more short-time acquaintances than long. I have had people in my life that just helped me pay off my bills and then the relationship died. I have had a person come in my life just to realize that I was unappreciative of the people that were in my life. I almost lost my life to a relationship. Yet, we wonder why some do not believe that God was with us even before we accepted His Call.

Let me start here. Do you know the meaning of your name? Seems like a crazy question. Are you thinking, it's not important? Are you thinking I never knew or thought about it? Well, do you believe that your journey started the day your parents named you? Whether intentional or not your name can give or take life.

Minister Amira challenged me to look at some things that were happening in my life. The first thing on the list was to find out what my name meant. It was not until I became serious about writing this book that I really understood that the enemy had taken this and used it against me this whole time. I was lacking knowledge.

My name is Persian and it means "sacred" or "sacred woman." Let us break this down: sacred, holy, cherished, blessed, spiritual and godly just to name a few words to put "sacred" into perspective. Wow, I thought. Now, what does this have to do with my life and trusting God? I was lacking knowledge because I know that Christ has had a plan for my life and the truth about me lies in the name. Do not go comparing your name to the Name of Jesus; there is none higher than His. But, doesn't it make sense that the enemy would try to keep me depressed, molested, and physically abused in order to keep me from obtaining or reaching for the goal that God had intended for me? Can you see that the more I isolate myself the more I continue to fall for the thoughts that I know keep me bound?

I needed to trust God in my dry places in order to see the land that was filled bountifully. The Word says, "the Lord bestows favor and honor. No good thing does he withhold from those who walk uprightly" Psalms 84:11. It is important that I get it right. I need to follow His instruction and ask Him for the steps of the blueprint so that I can reach my destiny. I have missed some blessings along the way; however, I am praying that some of those things He will restore and make available to me again. Trust God and get understanding. If we want to walk out this faith walk, we must trust God's plan. This is why you will hear me say, "I have made mistakes." I need God to help put me on track and give me the next step. I cannot do anything alone, but mess up His plan.

Every time Moses tried and did some things according to how the people were feeling, he messed it up. People were dying out there. What Moses did out there, alone, was because he did not trust God. I was dying out here because I wanted to do what I wanted to do! It is evident that alone without Christ, just won't work. Jesus died for us for our sins, but we keep getting in the way of our deliverance by allow the things we see or hear with our natural eyes and ears to distort the plans of God. Trust God. I do not want to be like Moses, and just tell people there is a promise land and not even I get an opportunity to see it. I must trust God!

I have seen people die because they just do not want to try anything new, even when the writing on the walls say, "danger, danger, and go back before it is too late." The message is clear, trust God. Trusting God, let's look at this a bit more. Trusting is having hope, faith, confidence, assurance and expectation in God, the ultimate authority, He is omnipotent. Why would we not want access to an unlimited, unrestricted Being, One possessing power that can heal and deliver?

Do not die before you reach your potential in Him.

Quick Prayer

Father, I come to You asking You to guard my heart from any more pain due to my own mistakes. I ask that You would allow me to see the mistakes and learn to depend on You. Allow

God my hope to be in You. Father, guard my eyes and my ears that the enemy would not speak or show me anything that is not of You. Keep my heart pure O God and allow me to love on You for just giving me another chance. It's in Jesus' Mighty Name I pray, Amen.

Trusting God Scriptures

Psalm 56:3
Psalm 91:1-2
Psalm 121:3

Ask Yourself?

So, we are almost there. What are you thinking about? Answer the following questions:

1. What does my life look like now? In your journal, describe one thing in your life that you find to be a major issue. While in my process of going-through, there were certain things that I did not like about myself. I had to think about those things and deal with them. For me, it was the molestation: I wanted and I did not want to know how I felt about it. I needed to know what I had contributed at that time good or bad and I had to deal with it. You need to deal with your issues, too. You know what people say about you, but what is true? Be honest with yourself. Your journaling is for you.

2. Now that God is showing you who you really are, how are you handling the situation? Are you getting help from your support team? Are you getting advice from other Christians or are you being prideful? What is the Lord telling you that you need to do about your situation? Stop watching TV; pray in the morning; help a neighbor? What are you doing to help you get through this tough time? For me, it started with my attitude. I did not like who I was, or who I was becoming. I saw myself walking around with an attitude, and wondering why I was so

miserable. Yes, it was because of the things I been through, but I had to make a decision. Should I stay in that mental place or move on with my life? What should I do about all the people I brought into my life? I chose to move forward.

3. Do you see yourself getting to your breakthrough? You must visualize success.

4. What are my goals in moving forward? I knew that I could not do this alone or with the same worldly people in my life. I have to set goals in order to change my way of living, and you do, too. I decided to go back to school. I had to cut back my TV watching and read my bible more. It was not just for me but necessary in order to reach the goals. I found that when I built up a tolerance to get rid of one thing, it has no room to come back in.

5. Will there be setbacks? Yes, I stopped drinking and cussing for 10 years. Then one day for some reason, I thought it was okay to take a drink. It set me back not only when I stopped the drinking, but also it made other things hard in my life. Like the people, I was influencing; you cannot be a person that constantly makes the same mistakes. You are stronger now because you have the great gift of the Holy Spirit Who guides and leads us in the right direction. We hear the voice of the enemy and get confused. Nevertheless, after you have been in your Word long enough, you will find out that not only is there hope but you are also a conqueror. (Philippians 4:13)

Ask Yourself?

Quick Prayer

Father God, I want to be a leader ready for Your command. God help me to retain what is needed in Your Word that will edify Your Kingdom and make me an example of You. I want to be transformed into the man/woman of God You have ordained me to be. Thank You Lord for Your loving kindness and Your grace and mercy You have given me. Let me not take this life for granted so that I can spend eternity with You in Your glorious Kingdom. In Jesus' Name I pray, Amen.

How to Maintain Self-discipline

Self-Discipline is just another word for *determination*. What defines determination? How desperate are you to getting your deliverance? Do you want to be obedient to the One Who knew you before you were born, and knows your ending? Whose goal are you looking to accomplish? Only what we do for Christ will matter and last.

We all have something that motivates us to want to be closer to Christ. Remember, we have done it and have been doing it our way. We still have a long way to go to not only bring a smile to God's face, but also keep Him smiling. We can only do this when we are on the same page with the Lord.

Yes, you have received Christ, but there is still work to do. That means you have to get your hands dirty and your feet wet at times. I mean just because you pray to God and want Him to reveal some things to you; it will still take your obedience to get the work completed. If you plan to work with children, you have to know how to tell if one requires a lot of your time and if another is feeling lonely, or when they are not themselves, etc. Everyday life will be like that for you, also. You must know that in order to grow out of your own ways you have to fill yourself up with more and more of Christ. This means praying daily and journaling to remember the things God will speak to you. You must read the Word of God to get the revelation of where God is taking you and your purpose for the task. We want to interpret things from our natural eyes and doing so will cause us to miss it, every time. But in using our spiritual eyes, it helps us to understand that at times we are given an assignment we can only fulfill when we trust God for His plan for His work.

Self-Discipline knows when to sacrifice. If you were on the brink of losing your family because of an addiction, would that motivate you to get clean? If you knew that hanging out with certain people would cause you to backslide or fall back into your old habits and ways, would that motivate you to distance yourself?

I can tell you that from a personal standpoint I had to distance myself from my family. I was falling into a system of alcoholism where I would drink every week from Thursday night to Saturday night; I was drinking according to my work schedule. My weekend would start on Thursday nights. I gave myself all of Sunday to get rid of the headaches and a chance to get some

How to Maintain Self-discipline

rest. At first, I really did not see it as a problem, but that was just the beginning. The problem developed when we think that we have it all under control. Everyone would like to think that it is not that bad when he or she is looking at himself or herself. "It's not that bad," I thought, but it really is if someone else brings it to your attention. God showed this to me. He said "you are turning into a weekend alcoholic" and I was! Every weekend, I continued to do the same thing. I had to be accountable for what I was doing. So, after I got married, I began to separate myself from my family because I felt that if I went around them I would lose all self-discipline. And at times, I did. I would visit them, and not bring anything to ensure I would not drink. As much as I would say that I was not going to drink anything... there would always be something available. Free.

So, do not let anything keep you from being strong. Strength comes from the Word of God. This is why we should read the bible daily. I know now that it is okay to be around my family and limit my time if everyone is drinking. I am not condemning anyone. Let us talk about when you have family that talks about you behind your back (so they think) and someone else is Facebooking it or calling you with the "Did you know?" syndrome. You have family calling you talking about "Girl if you leave your husband nobody is going to be mad at you." Satan got you thinking, "Do they know something that I don't know?" Do you really need an audience at your wedding when the very people that call themselves family are hoping for the worse for your marriage? That moment is special between you, your spouse and the Lord. Sometimes, we miss this point in getting married and may suffer for it throughout. I am just being accountable for my weaknesses. Can you be honest about the contribution you made in my life or someone else's life you are setting up to fail? Because the reality is that if I am a mess, I am setting up someone else to fail, too! Especially, if I am not getting the help I need.

It is not that I do not love my family. At that time, God needed me in a place to receive my deliverance and my healing. If I did not choose to be alone with God, I would not have realized why I was so angry, and start dealing with my anger and bitterness. I would never have known that incest was making me sad and depressed. I would not have been able to understand that being in an abusive domestic relationship caused me to be bitter and insecure in my marriage. Every time he goes to touch me in a certain way, it sets me off. Telling me he is doing one thing, but I needed to be sure he was. My husband is telling me he loves me, but in my mind, I am thinking the worse. I would not have been able to see that our youngest son was suffering from depression. Do not let anybody tell you that you cannot be lonely in a house full of people! The world isolates us and we isolate the very ones we love. We need you, Lord!

Before I married, it was just my sister and me. Even she would act out because our daddy was gone. So do not tell me that single parent households do not matter because they do! But, what are we doing to help that family that is suffering? Did I want to see my mother and father fight? Although I did not have any children, the process would be passed down to the next generation; passed down through insecurity, loneliness, and bad spending habits. And you still may be wondering what does this have to do with self-discipline and salvation?!

If you have self-discipline, you know that you can call on Him to stop you from acting out in your time of weakness because the Word of God lives in you. The Name of Jesus can cause that urge for chocolate, food, drugs, smoking, alcohol, unfaithfulness, filthy sexual desires and pornography to flee.

God wants us to have a life flowing with His goodness. We are striving for righteousness and holiness, and we cannot do it without self-discipline. In order to stop passing down negativity we have to stop with our foolishness. Even our slang is ruining our children (profanity in Rap, Spoken Word, and song lyrics). We should be able to have fun and enjoy each other. But, we cannot because we do not know how to live with Christ. We need Him! He desires to have your full attention! It's not about being ready it's about sacrifice.

When the enemy tries to take your thoughts into the land of unforgiveness and bitterness, do not let him. STOP! Recite a scripture and remind yourself that you are a child of the Most High God, and that no devil in hell can take what he does not own. If you did or didn't know, let me remind you that the Word of God says that we are able to cast down thoughts and imaginations of every high thing that exalted itself against the knowledge of God. You need to read and keep I Corinthians 10:5 close to your heart in order to put the devil in his place.

"Be sober, be vigilant; because your adversary the devil walks about like a roaring lion, seeking whom he can devour. Resist him, steadfast in the faith, knowing that the same sufferings are experienced by your brotherhood in the world. But, may the God of all grace, who called us to His eternal glory by Christ

Jesus, after you have suffered a while, perfect, establish, strengthen, and settle you." (I Peter 5:8-10)

Quick Prayer

Father, thank You Lord for helping me understand that I am nothing without You. Thank You, Father, that You desire to be there for me in my weakest hour. Thank You in advance Father for showing me who I am in You and not who the world tries to mold me to be. The song simply says that You are the potter and we are the clay. Thank You, Jesus, for intervening and changing me in those times when self-discipline was not known. Thank You that You are going to show me in my quieter times who You desire me to be in You. Help me Lord to develop such a strong relationship with You that it will cause every area of my life to be clean. Thank You, Lord and Savior, for even giving me the time to make it right. Thank You Father, in Jesus' Name, Amen.

Scripture for Tough Times

"In order for our spirit to be rich, we must take on a new rich spirit, which is in Christ Jesus." Ephesians 2:18

"Trust in the Lord with all your heart, and lean not on your own understanding; In all your ways acknowledge Him, and He shall direct your paths. Do not be wise in your own eyes; fear the Lord and depart from evil. It will be health to your flesh, and strength to your bones." Proverbs 3:5-8

"The Lord is my light and my salvation; whom shall I fear? The Lord is strength of my life; of whom shall I be afraid? When the enemy came against me to eat up my flesh, my enemies and foes, they stumbled and fell. Though an army may encamp against me, my heart shall not fear; though war may rise against me, in this I will be confident." Psalm 27:1-3

Fight for It...Just Get to Him!

What you did not know about me is that I suffer from panic attacks. Panic attacks for me are brought on by disobedience. Many people can relate to this because of fear of things like snakes, being in a crowd of people, etc.... Yeah, me too, but I also go through this as I try to get closer to God. The more I read my bible and the more I pray over and for my family I have panic attacks. However, did you know that panic attacks happen just like any other attack of the enemy? When you least expect it! I have been in the emergency room more times than I have fingers and toes to count them on.

I knew that I was drawing closer to God because of the attacks on my family were stronger than ever. The things we could usually handle seemed far from our reach. Tempers were short and attitudes were at an all-time high. Our children were going nuts. We had to get it together! We began praying together in the morning and we were improving after a few months; I could see God moving. But, the panic attacks came, anytime, anywhere. At first, I did not understand, but when they seemed like heart attacks, I prayed harder and just kept calling on the Name of Jesus. Proverbs 18:10 says, "The name of the Lord is a strong tower; the righteous runneth into it, and is safe." I am telling you how to be safe, no enemy wants to come face to face with that Name. They know it holds power and strength. Our job is to rely on that power to receive our strength. I am so excited to be able to share with you the goodness of Jesus. It was a long road.

I am glad that the Lord is so desirable; His Greatness keeps me coming back every time. I want you to know that this journey gets rough and you can make it with the Lord on your side. We are in a time now that we can expect the unexpected. Our government may have been built on Christ, but even as Christians, we do sometimes lose our way. But, God is waiting on you to take our salvation seriously. He wants you to come to Him and pray, meditate and listen for His Voice. He is waiting for you to make the next move. Do not let this be another thing that falls by the wayside. Do this because you realize that you are nothing without Him. He makes all things new.

"The Spirit of the Sovereign LORD is on me, because the LORD has anointed me to proclaim good news to the poor. He has sent me to bind up the brokenhearted, to proclaim freedom for the captives and release from darkness for the prisoners, to proclaim the year of the LORD's favor and the day of vengeance of our God, to comfort all who mourn, and provide for those who grieve in Zion—to bestow on them a crown of beauty instead of ashes, the oil of joy instead of mourning, and a garment of praise instead of a spirit of despair.

They will be called oaks of righteousness, a planting of the LORD for the display of his splendor" (Isaiah 61:1-3).

I pray that you have been enlightened and that you will fight to be before the Lord your God. He wants you to prosper and be a blessing to others. Do not give up, but run like never before, and know how great our God is. We must take part in our miracle and not wait for it to just appear. To God Be the Glory!

Citations

1.] Dictionary.com
    a. Salvation
    http://dictionary.reference.com/browse/salvation?s=t
    b. Easton 1897 Bible Dictionary
    http://dictionary.reference.com/browse/salvation?s=t
    (bottom of the page.)
2.] Thomas Nelson Publishers. (1982). Nelson's three-in-one Bible reference companion. Nashville: T. Nelson.
    a. Page 605
    b. Repent   Page 508
3.] The Holy Bible: King James version. (2010). Peabody, Mass: Hendrickson Bibles.
4.] Dictionary.com.
5.] Easton's 1897 Bible Dictionary.
    http://dictionary.reference.com/browse/graft (accessed: November 14, 2013).
6.] Healing Rejection & Emotional Abuse by Jonas Clark 2011
7.] YouVersion.com

About the Author

Hello everyone! I am a lover of Christ, wife, mother, daughter, sister, grandmother, author, radio personality, inspirational writer. I have been in Christ for many years but not really tapping into His fullness. I am a wife of 16 years; God has blessed me with a great man who has stuck by me since the first day we met. We have been through a lot in our marriage and with Christ we have been able to bounce back and reconnect, not only with our love but our love for Christ.

For me, my personal journey has been long or should I say prolonged by the fear of the unknown. I have been through incest, domestic violence, homelessness, embarrassment, guilt, shame, lied on, lied too and the list goes on. I use to be a big sufferer of depression and panic attacks. I suffered from insecurity and lack of trust in people. I felt like I was drowning in sea of shame and guilt. My awesome Bishop preached a series on DO IT NOW in 2015. It is still ringing in my soul today. I am motivated by his words of inspiration and desperation to save the lives of others, not just close friends and family but, especially people who feel they have no one.

www.ingramcontent.com/pod-product-compliance
Lightning Source LLC
Chambersburg PA
CBHW070547300426
44113CB00011B/1819